P9-DMY-196

Real Stories From My Time

Melody™

THE
MARCH ON
WASHINGTON

By Bonnie Bader

With Melody Stories by Denise Lewis Patrick

Illustrated by Kelley McMorris

Scholastic Inc.

Published by Scholastic Inc., *Publishers since 1920*. SCHOLASTIC and associated logos are trademarks and/or registered trademarks of Scholastic Inc. The publisher does not have any control over and does not assume any responsibility for author or third-party websites or their content.

Photos ©: back cover: Robert W. Kelley/Getty Images; 2: Everett Collection Historical/Alamy Stock Photo; 10: The Granger Collection; 12: Stan Wayman/Getty Images; 23: Rex Hardy Jr./Getty Images; 30: Carl Iwasaki/Getty Images; 33: Underwood Archives/UIG/Shutterstock; 35: Don Cravens/Getty Images; 37: The Granger Collection; 47: Everett Collection Inc/Alamy Stock Photo; 49: Bettmann/Getty Images; 57: Associated Press/AP Images; 59: The Granger Collection; 66: Hulton Archive/Getty Images; 69: Bettmann/Getty Images; 78: Associated Press/AP Images; 87: John F. Kennedy Presidential Library and Museum, Boston; 89: Robert W. Kelley/Getty Images; 92: Rowland Scherman/Getty Images; 102: Historia/Shutterstock; 103: Hulton Archive/Getty Images.

Speech excerpt on page 90 reprinted by arrangement with The Heirs to the Estate of Martin Luther King Jr., c/o Writers House as agent for the proprietor New York, NY. © 1963 Dr. Martin Luther King, Jr. © renewed 1991 Coretta Scott King.

Illustrated by Kelley McMorris
Book design by Suzanne M. LaGasa
Special thanks to Jevon Bolden

americangirl.com/service

ISBN 978-1-338-19301-5

10 9 8 7 6 5 4 3 2 1   19 20 21 22 23

Printed in the U.S.A. 23

First printing 2019

For Lauren and Allie—may you always stand up, and march, for what is right. —B.B.

America's past is filled with stories of courage, adventure, hardship, and hope. The Real Stories From My Time series pairs American Girl's beloved historical characters with true stories of pivotal events in American history. As you travel back in time to discover America's past, these characters share their own incredible tales with you.

CONTENTS

A Note About Language

Throughout the 1900s, the terms *Negro, colored,* and *black* were all used to describe Americans of African descent. You'll see all of those words used in this book.

Today, *Negro* and *colored* can be offensive because they are associated with racial inequality. The term *African American* wasn't commonly used until the late 1980s.

Chapter 1

A March toward Freedom

On August 28, 1963, more than two hundred and fifty thousand people poured into the capital of the United States: Washington, DC. They came in cars and buses. They rode in vans and trucks. They pedaled bicycles and revved the engines of motorcycles. They walked—some more than two hundred miles. And they sang:

We shall overcome
We shall overcome
We shall overcome, some day

They came to protest the unfair treatment of black people in the United States. At that time, black children went to separate schools. Black adults couldn't freely vote. Black people could not sit with white people on buses or in movie theaters or restaurants. They couldn't live in certain neighborhoods or be hired for certain jobs because of the color of their skin. The marchers wanted the United States government to pass laws that would give black people the same opportunities as white people.

Peaceful protesters carry signs in the March on Washington

People of all ages, from every part of the country, gathered to march for equality for black people. Fifteen-year-old Ericka Jenkins lived in Washington, DC. As the protesters passed her home, she didn't just watch them go by. She joined them. She marched through her neighborhood toward the National Monument, where a large group was gathering. "I saw people laughing and listening and standing very close to one another, almost in an embrace," she wrote. "Children of every size, pregnant women, elderly people who seemed tired but happy to be there."

The protesters were not just African Americans. People of all races joined the march, raising their voices in song, listening to speeches, and standing together to demand that the government take action. But what did it take for all these people to come together in Washington for this historic event? More than one hundred years of protests, demonstrations, **boycotts**, sit-ins, and court cases all led up to this powerful moment in history.

In 1963, Melody Ellison was a nine-year-old girl growing up in Detroit, Michigan. She loved music, and she was thrilled to be chosen to sing a solo at church. But she was nervous, too. Melody wasn't used to singing all by herself, so she asked her brother, Dwayne, for advice. He was a talented musician who was determined to become a famous singer. Melody was also interested in what her college-age sister, Yvonne, had to say about equal rights for black people. And she was curious about the stories her parents and grandparents told about being treated unfairly.

Melody knew what **racism** felt like. She faced **discrimination** herself, and she decided that she had to speak up about inequality. She attended the Walk to Freedom, where she was inspired by the size of the crowds and by the words of Dr. Martin Luther King Jr. As Melody discovered how long and hard black people had been working for justice and equality, she was proud to add her voice to the **civil rights** movement in America.

The 1960s was a time of great struggle, but also of great hope. Across the country, well-known leaders and ordinary citizens—including children like Melody—took action on important issues. They worked together, kept one another strong, and changed history.

Although Melody is a fictional character, her story will help you imagine what it was like to live during the civil rights movement of the 1960s.

We Are Americans

My grandfather shakes his head. "It's a shame that colored people today still have to be afraid of standing up or speaking out for themselves."

"Negroes," Mommy corrects him.

"Black people," my oldest sister, Yvonne, says firmly.

"Well, what are we supposed to call ourselves?" my other sister, Lila, asks.

I think about how our grandparents usually say *colored*. They're older and from the South, and our grandmother says that's what was proper when they were growing up. Mommy and Daddy mostly say *Negroes*. But ever since she went to college, Yvonne is saying *black*

6

people. I notice that Mommy and Daddy are saying it sometimes, too. I speak up. "What about Americans?" I say.

"That's right, Dee Dee." Yvonne nods. "We're Americans. We have the same rights as white Americans. There shouldn't be any separate water fountains or waiting rooms or public bathrooms. Black Americans deserve equal treatment and equal pay. And sometimes we have to remind people."

"How do we remind them?" Lila asks. I was wondering the same thing.

"By not shopping at stores that won't hire black workers," Yvonne explains. "By picketing in front of restaurants that won't serve black people. By marching."

Yvonne's voice is strong and certain. She stands up for what she believes in, I think. I'm proud she's my sister, and I hope I can be as brave as she is.

Chapter 2

Jim Crow Laws

The United States of America became a country in 1776 with the signing of the Declaration of Independence. The document states that "all men are created equal." But this statement did not apply to everyone. At the time, most black people in America were enslaved, and they were not considered equal to white people.

The first enslaved people were brought to Jamestown, Virginia, in 1619 from Africa. They were forced to work without pay. Many families were torn apart when children were sold away from parents. These enslaved people had no rights at all.

By 1861, the country was deeply divided over many issues, including slavery. The Civil War broke out, and over the next four years, soldiers from the Northern states (the Union army) and Southern states (the Confederate army) fought one another.

In 1863, President Abraham Lincoln issued the **Emancipation Proclamation**, which declared all people enslaved in

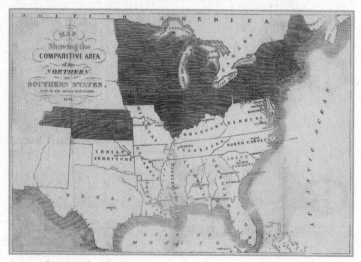

A map showing the Northern states (in gray) and Southern states (in white), 1861

Confederate states free. But people in the South ignored the proclamation. The war—and slavery—continued. It wasn't until 1865, after the war ended, that black people who had been enslaved in America officially became citizens. But being free did not mean that black people were treated the same as white people. **Prejudice** and racism still existed, especially in the South. From the 1870s through the 1950s, some states created laws that **segregated**, or separated, black people from white people.

Black people were not allowed into many hotels, stores, and hospitals. Many restaurants and theaters had separate doors and seating areas for black people. Public buildings had separate drinking fountains, often marked "white" and "colored." Black people had to ride in the back of the bus. Black and white children went to separate schools. Schools for black children usually had fewer books and supplies than schools for white children, and the buildings were often in poor condition. If black people did not follow the laws, they could face punishment—including jail time or even death. Living under these conditions was very frightening for black people in the South.

A segregated bus in 1956

All of these rules were part of the **Jim Crow laws**. The term comes from a fictional character of that name. When a white performer dressed up as Jim Crow, he would darken his face with charcoal and make fun of black people. "Jim Crow" is a negative way of talking about black people, and Jim

Crow laws unfairly segregated black people from white people. The fear of being punished for breaking these laws controlled nearly every part of a black person's life.

Jim Crow laws did not exist in the northern states, but black people living there still faced segregation and discrimination. They could be refused services in stores, restaurants, and hospitals. They were not given equal chances to get jobs. Often a white candidate would be hired over a black candidate even if the black candidate had the same qualifications. It was difficult for black people to buy houses in certain neighborhoods—especially if the neighborhood was mostly white.

But when a black person from the North visited the South, they had to follow Jim Crow laws. Richard Hill lived in St. Louis, Missouri. When he was five or six, his mother took him and his brothers to Mississippi to visit their grandmother. His mother had told her boys about the segregation laws in the South.

Richard thought they were just stories. But in Mississippi, he realized that his mother was telling the truth! It was a huge shock. Richard later said that his mom told him that he could be anything he wanted, "but that I'd have to work three or four times harder to get it, whereas a white person, just being white was their free admission." Visiting the South helped Richard understand what his mother meant.

Black people faced many challenges trying to vote for politicians who would help change these unfair laws. In some southern states, black people were charged a poll tax. This meant that they had to pay money to vote. A lot of black people couldn't afford the fee, and without it, they could not cast their ballot. Most white people did not have to pay the poll tax.

In other southern states, black people often had to pass a **literacy** test to vote. The test was given by a white person, who could make the test as hard as they wanted. John

Lewis, a black American politician and civil rights leader, recalled, "On one occasion, a man was asked to count how many bubbles on a bar of soap." White people voted without having to pass any kind of test.

The Jim Crow laws restricted life for black people in the South. Under these laws, black people did not have the same rights as white people. In the North, black people did not have equal rights, either. Something had to be done to fix these injustices!

A Lasting Memory

Once when I was only four, my grandparents took me south. It was very hot, and the lemonade in Big Momma's thermos was gone. I was still thirsty, so when Poppa stopped at a gas station in Alabama, I begged for a drink. There was a Coca-Cola machine, red and white and shiny. Poppa gave me a nickel so that I could buy an ice-cold soda pop. Big Momma walked me to the machine, but when we got closer, she said, "Stop, baby."

"I want a drink!" I said.

"I know," Big Momma said, "but we can't today. The machine is broken. Put your money in your pocket now."

Big momma took my hand to guide me away, and I followed her back to the car. That's when a little blonde girl about my size went to the machine. She stood on tiptoe and dropped a coin in. Then she reached in and pulled a frosty bottle out of the machine.

"It's not broken!" I shouted. "It's not! I want a soda pop, too!" I cried, pulling against Big momma's arm. But she put me back in the car, and we drove away. I remember crying for a long time.

It wasn't until I was older and could read that I understood. A few years later we were again driving south and stopped at a station, this time in Tennessee. I got out to stretch my legs, and I saw the same kind of soda machine. There was a sign above the machine that said, "Whites

Only." That's when I realized that the machine in Alabama must have had the same kind of sign.

When I asked Big Momma why she hadn't told me about the sign the first time, she said, "Because it hurt me too much. I didn't want it to hurt you, too."

Chapter 3

A Movement Begins

For black people, speaking out against unfair treatment was an enormous risk—especially in the South. They could be arrested or lose their jobs. Their homes could be destroyed. They could be beaten or even killed for standing up for their rights.

But while it was dangerous, many brave black men and women did speak out and challenge this treatment. In the early 1900s, they created new groups and organizations to challenge racist laws. The most famous of these organizations was the National

Association for the Advancement of Colored People (NAACP), founded in 1909. The NAACP had both black and white leaders who worked to improve the lives of black people throughout the United States.

Other people worked to improve the lives of black people, too, such as A. Philip Randolph, who founded an organization for black railroad porters. Porters were workers who took care of passengers on overnight train trips. When the Brotherhood of Sleeping Car Porters was founded in 1925, it was one of the first times that black workers had a **union**, a group that fought and spoke out for their fair treatment. In 1937, after protesting unfair conditions for black porters, the Brotherhood got the workers more money, shorter working hours, and better working conditions. Randolph and the members of the union learned that organizing and protesting could change an unfair situation.

Inspired by the Brotherhood's success, Randolph decided to try and protest in other

A. Philip Randolph speaks to the railroad porters in 1937

ways. When World War II broke out, he realized that there would be new jobs in the
defense industry. Most companies that made
equipment and supplies for the military had
"whites only" hiring policies. Randolph
decided to lead a march to protest this discrimination. He and other organizers spread
the word in barbershops, grocery stores, and

local businesses. At first, ten thousand people were expected to attend, but the number quickly swelled to over one hundred thousand! The march was scheduled to take place July 1, 1941. But a week before the march, President Franklin D. Roosevelt issued an order prohibiting discrimination in the defense industry. Just *planning* a march had been enough to create change! Black Americans saw that their voices could be heard when they joined together.

By the end of the war, black people had learned how to organize and how to spread their message. They knew how powerful protests could be. They were starting a movement in the United States. This movement was not about violence. It was about justice. It was peaceful. It was organized. It became known as the civil rights movement.

That's Not Fair

After school, I hold Mommy's hand as we walk through the lobby of Detroit Bank. We're the only black people in sight, and I'm the only child. As we stand in a short line, I feel uncomfortable. I take a deep breath and remind myself that I'm standing up for my sister—and for making things fair.

When it's my turn, I let go of Mommy's hand and step up to the counter. I make myself as tall as I can. The bank teller is an older white woman with red hair. "I would like to withdraw my money," I tell her.

"And how much would you like to withdraw?" the teller asks.

"All of it," I tell her.

The teller raises her eyebrows. "Are you sure?" she asks kindly.

"Yes," I say firmly. "My sister is really good with money and numbers, but this bank wouldn't let her apply for a summer job because she's black. That's not fair."

The teller looks confused for a moment. "Do you understand, dear, that if you withdraw everything you'll close your account?" I see her glance over my head in Mommy's direction.

I slide my bankbook across the counter. My insides are quivering a little, but I look straight at the teller. "Yes. I understand. This bank discriminates against black people. I don't want to keep my money here anymore."

Chapter 4

Brown and Boycotts

At the end of World War II, African Americans were newly energized. They had the unions and the organizers to lead them. The NAACP focused their efforts in court and worked to improve the lives of African Americans by changing the law.

In the 1950s, the NAACP challenged America's segregated school system. When several black parents to tried to enroll their children in their local school, they were not allowed because the schools were for white children only. They were told that their

29

children had to go to black schools instead, even though the white schools were closer. One of the children, Linda Brown, was a black third grader living in Topeka, Kansas. To get to the all-black school, Linda had to walk six blocks, cross railroad tracks, and then take a two-mile bus ride to school. Linda's father and the NAACP sued the Topeka Board

Linda Brown in front of Monroe Elementary School, the all-black school she had to travel to every day

of Education. The case—*Brown v. Board of Education of Topeka, Kansas*—went all the way up to the highest court in the United States: the Supreme Court.

Thurgood Marshall, a lawyer who later became the first black Supreme Court Justice, argued the side of Brown. Marshall showed that separating children by color was unequal. Marshall demanded a change to the law. When it came time for the nine Supreme Court Justices—all of whom were white men—to vote on the case in 1954, they all voted against school segregation. Black and white children across the United States could now legally go to the same school.

The success of the *Brown* court case gave African Americans the momentum to challenge segregation in other areas. In 1955, fifteen-year-old Claudette Colvin was riding home on a city bus in Montgomery, Alabama. At school, Claudette's class had been studying the Constitution and the Bill of Rights. Her teacher helped her to understand her rights as an American citizen. When the bus driver told Claudette to give up her seat to a white passenger, Claudette refused. "It's my constitutional right to sit here as much as that lady," Claudette said.

Claudette saw that she was being treated unfairly. But more importantly, she realized that she could do something to change the unfair system. Though she was scared, Claudette remained seated. Her peaceful refusal to follow the unjust law is an example of **civil disobedience**. Claudette was dragged off the bus and thrown in jail. "I was really afraid, because you just didn't know what white people might do at that time," she said. Later that same year, eighteen-year-old Mary Louise Smith followed Claudette's lead. She refused to give up her bus seat. Like Claudette, she was thrown in jail. They were only teenagers, but they were brave enough to make a stand.

Although Claudette's and Mary Louise's cases did not receive national attention, a similar case did. On December 1, 1955, Rosa Parks was riding a Montgomery city bus on her way home from work. She was seated in the "colored" section at the back. As more and more passengers got on, the bus became crowded. The bus driver told Rosa to give up her seat for a white man. Rosa refused, and was arrested and jailed. It was not the first time that Rosa Parks had refused to follow

A police officer takes Rosa Parks's fingerprints

the rules on the bus, but it was the first time she had been arrested.

Upon hearing about Rosa Parks's arrest, a local group called the Women's Political Council decided to stage a one-day boycott of the Montgomery city buses. The group asked black people not to ride any buses on Monday, December 5. They made flyers that explained Rosa Parks's arrest and said, "This has to be stopped. Negroes have rights, too, for if Negroes did not ride the buses, they could not operate." In other words, without black customers, the bus company would lose money. The boycott was a form of **economic protest**.

It was very difficult for black Americans to stop using the bus. Many of them didn't have cars and they needed to get to work, but they knew that they had to be strong to create change. Instead of lasting just one day, the boycott lasted more than a year. Black people in Montgomery formed a group called the Montgomery Improvement Association

(MIA), and they chose twenty-six-year-old Dr. Martin Luther King Jr., a preacher, to be their leader. They developed a careful plan to keep the boycott going. Dr. King and the MIA organized car pools so that people could get to work. Every night the black community met in King's church to sing and listen to speeches. They showed one another that they were not alone. By working as a team, they created a movement.

A carpool during the Montgomery bus boycott

Without black riders, the bus company lost between thirty and forty thousand fares each day. By January the bus company was nearly broke—the economic protest was working! In 1956, the Supreme Court made segregated buses illegal. After 381 days of boycotting, Montgomery's African American community celebrated their win. It was a major victory for the civil rights movement. Black Americans felt empowered to push for more change.

The bus boycott showed young African Americans that they could use their voices and fight for fairer conditions in their towns. Many college students began to think about what they could do to change the world around them. All over the country, black students started their own economic protests. The most famous one began on February 1, 1960, in Greensboro, North Carolina. Four black college students sat down at the lunch counter in a Woolworth's store and asked for coffee. The lunch counter was for whites only, so the waitress refused to serve them. The four students didn't move. When they were asked to leave, they refused. They were all afraid, but they stayed on their stools until the store closed.

Black teenagers sit at the Woolworth's counter in Greensboro, North Carolina, 1960

Stories of their protest quickly spread around campus. The next day they returned with twenty-three of their classmates. The day after that, the students occupied sixty-three of the sixty-five seats at the Woolworth's counter. On the fourth day, one hundred students filled the store. With every seat occupied by a black person, the lunch counter could not make any money. The students were using an economic protest—the same technique they had seen in the Montgomery bus boycott—to create change.

The students knew they had to be organized, so they arranged the sit-ins in shifts. They created training schools to teach other students how to protest peacefully. White and black students joined the cause, and within two months the sit-in movements had spread to fifty-four cities in nine states. The students had to be very brave. As they sat at lunch counters across the country, they were often attacked by angry white crowds. Some white people shouted at them, others threw food and drinks at them, and some hit them. But still the students remained seated and did not fight back.

Afraid of the violence, many white customers avoided downtown stores, and black customers boycotted them. Without customers, stores in the South were in serious trouble. But the boycott did not impact just southern stores. In the North, people protested outside of Woolworth's stores and boycotted the stores in support of students in the South. Woolworth's was very concerned about losing money. On July 25, 1960, they agreed to desegregate the lunch counters. Once again, protesters had used the "power of the purse" to create change.

Boycott!

Once a month, several families from my neighborhood get together for a meeting of the Block Club. Us kids play games while our parents talk about what's going on in Detroit and in the community. Tonight I'm in the kitchen playing dominoes with my friends when I hear something from the living room that makes me want to listen.

"I tell you, we need to do something about the new management at Fieldston's Clothing Store," someone says. "They're in the middle of a Negro community, but they act as if every Negro customer is there to steal something!"

"That's not right," my father says.

Without thinking, I open the door wide and barge into the living room. "Fieldston's does discriminate against black people!" I say, walking into the middle of the circle of chairs.

All eyes turn toward me. "And how do you know that?" Mrs. Harris asks, surprised.

"I know because the manager accused me of shoplifting," I say. "I don't think we should spend our money in a store that treats us like that."

My father starts nodding. "I've heard that same story over and over. I think we ought to protest by boycotting Fieldston's."

"You mean not shop there at all?" Mrs. Harris says.

"Yes," Daddy answers. "And I say we picket in front of the store, too. We can hand out leaflets that explain how they

41

treat black customers. They may not want to notice us, but they notice our money. And they'll notice when it's gone."

The grown-ups keep talking as I make my way back to the kitchen. All my friends stare at me.

"Do you really think people will boycott Fieldston's?" Diane Harris asks. "My mom shops there all the time."

"She won't be able to if there's a picket line in front of the store," I say.

All of a sudden, I make a decision. "I'm going to make a picket sign, and I'm going to carry it in the boycott. If my parents let me."

"Are you nuts?" Diane asks.

I shake my head. "This is about being fair. Maybe a boycott will make

Fieldston's change. Wouldn't that be better for everybody?"

"Mostly for our parents," Diane says.

"That's not true," I insist. "If our parents don't get treated fairly, we don't either. In the South a sign on a water fountain that says 'Whites Only' means grown-ups and kids. That's why kids have been standing up and marching for equal rights."

Diane nods slowly. "Maybe all of us kids should march."

Chapter 5

The World Is Watching

As the civil rights movement grew, television and newspapers reported on their efforts. Protesters realized that the media could be a very powerful tool. They looked for opportunities to capture America's racism on camera. They wanted the media to spread images of their struggle around the world.

In the summer of 1955, fourteen-year-old Emmett Till set off from Chicago to spend the summer with his cousins in Mississippi. As his mother kissed him good-bye, she warned him to be careful. For black boys like

Emmett, life in the South was very different from life in Chicago. Soon Emmett and his cousins were enjoying their time together. Emmett showed them photos of his school friends. Emmett's class had both white and black children, and his cousins had never seen anything like it! According to reports at that time, one day the cousins went to a store. As they left, Emmett said, "Bye, baby," to the young white lady serving him.

In the South, if a black person even looked at a white person in a way the white person didn't like, the black person could get into a lot of trouble. Four days after Emmett and his cousins visited the store, the young woman's husband and brother-in-law kidnapped Emmett. They beat him, shot him, and then threw his body in the river. When Emmett's body was found, it had been beaten so badly that he was unrecognizable.

At Till's funeral, Mamie Bradley, his mother, insisted on an open casket. She wanted the world to see what the white men

Emmett Till and his mother, circa 1950

had done to her boy. Magazines printed pictures of Emmett's body. One fifteen-year-old girl who saw those pictures said it gave her a new fear—"the fear of being killed just because I was black." Mamie Bradley had focused the eyes of the world on Mississippi, and now they saw how terrifying life could be for even young black people.

Two years later, images from another event once again opened America's eyes to racism. Although the *Brown* decision had made segregation illegal, many schools remained seg-regated. One of these schools was Central High School in Little Rock, Arkansas. In September 1957, the Little Rock School Board agreed to *slowly* start integrating their schools. But the NAACP knew that integration would not be easy. They selected nine black students who all had excellent grades—as well as great courage—to be the first black students at Central High School. Those students became known as the Little Rock Nine.

On the first day of school, the Little Rock Nine agreed to meet and go together. But somehow, one of the students didn't get the message. Elizabeth Eckford arrived at school alone. The fifteen-year-old faced a mob of several hundred angry white people. People shouted and spat at her. They even threat-ened to kill her. Elizabeth kept walking. She headed for the guards at the door. She thought they would help her, but they blocked her from the school. Elizabeth had no choice but to return home.

Elizabeth Eckford arriving on the first day of school

Reporters in Little Rock spread the story all over the world. One famous photo captured the moment that a young white student screamed at Elizabeth. People saw the images and were shocked by what was going on in America. Little Rock was no longer just a local issue. The photos made it a national problem.

The Little Rock Nine were very brave. They kept calm, even when other students got violent. They felt it was their right to attend Central High School. And a lot of people in America agreed. It was time to peacefully fight for change.

The Picket Line

At ten o'clock in the morning, a group gathers in front of Fieldston's. Even though it's cold, almost fifty people have shown up to protest. I stand in a line with my mother while my father walks among the people, passing out leaflets and protest signs. I've made my own sign. It says, "Support Our Boycott!" I'm ready to hold it up high and march.

Daddy picks up a sign. "Shop in dignity!" he chants, walking slowly along the sidewalk.

I get a good grip on my sign and begin to pick up the chant. At the corner past Fieldston's, the line crosses the street and marches on the other side. People turn their signs so that anyone looking out of the Fieldston's window can read them.

Many of the protesters look straight ahead when they walk past the Fieldston's window, but I can't. When I'm in front of the store, I turn to stare. I find myself looking right at the same man—the manager—who'd accused Dwayne and me of shoplifting. For a second our eyes lock.

Do you recognize me? I wonder. The man's face grows paler as he realizes that the line is not ending. The chanting is not stopping.

I keep my eyes on the window after I pass the store. I see a white man stop at the door. My father hands the man one of the leaflets. The man reads it, and then backs away and leaves without crossing the picket line.

Someone starts singing and I sing, too. I sing as loud as I can, becoming part of the rhythm of voices. I realize that because of my own experience at Fieldston's, I'm connected to people I'll never know: the people from the past who have been treated unfairly, just as I have been, and people in the future, who won't face this sort of discrimination. After all, if the boycott is a success, things will change.

At home that night, my legs are tired from walking, and my arms are tired from holding up my protest sign. But my heart feels stronger because I've been part of something I believe in. When our boycott makes the news on the radio, I feel like the whole world is listening.

Chapter 6

The Children's Crusade

By 1963, Martin Luther King realized how much power an image in the newspaper or on television could have. With a bold new plan, Dr. King headed to one of the most segregated cities in the South: Birmingham, Alabama.

Birmingham was controlled by a police commissioner called Eugene "Bull" Connor who was determined to keep his city segregated. King and leaders of his protest group, the Southern Christian Leadership Conference (SCLC), planned to confront Bull Connor and use the media to spread images of their struggle. They called the plan Project C. The *C* stood for confrontation.

In Birmingham, the SCLC set up headquarters in the Sixteenth Street Baptist Church. They led sit-ins, marched to city hall, and met with black community members. They held church services and sang freedom songs to unite people.

To try and stop the SCLC from protesting segregation, the city banned demonstrations. Anyone who protested would go to jail. The SCLC marched anyway. On April 12, protesters including Dr. King, were arrested. News cameras were there to capture the scene.

After Dr. King was released on April 20, he began preparing for the next stage of Project C. One of his advisers suggested they organize a children's march. Most young people didn't have jobs, so if they went to jail, they wouldn't be fired like their parents would. King was hesitant at first, but he

Dr. Martin Luther King Jr. is arrested on April 12, 1963

agreed. What happened next became known as the Children's Crusade.

King knew that children were impacted by racism, and he wanted to give them a chance to create change. The SCLC talked to black schoolchildren all over the city and encouraged them to join the march. Carolyn McKinstry was fourteen years old when she overheard talk at her church about a children's march. She could feel the excitement in the air and wanted to be part of it. But she didn't tell her parents. She knew they wouldn't want her to go. They would think it was too dangerous.

To prepare them for the march, organizers taught the children about sit-ins and how other young people had protested. On May 2, nearly one thousand black students stayed out of school and gathered at the Sixteenth Street Baptist Church. Some were as young as six years old. From the church, they took to the streets fifty at a time, singing as they marched toward downtown. They encountered police and were arrested. Yet, more children kept coming out of the church and peacefully marching. By the end of the day, 959 children had been taken to jail.

The next day, the children returned. But this time, Police Commissioner Bull Connor tried to stop them with ferocious police dogs that ripped their clothes and bit them. The police turned on fire hoses and some children were knocked to the ground from the force of the water. The water was so powerful that it tore bark off trees. The press was there to capture the horrible reality of racism.

A police dog attacks a black boy in Birmingham, 1963

Despite being beaten, bitten, hosed, and jailed, the children continued to march. Sixteen-year-old Jessie Shepherd was soaking wet when she was arrested. "I was told not to participate," she later said. "But I was tired of the injustice." Soon, Birmingham's jails were so overcrowded that the arrested students were brought to a local fairground. They slept on cots and sang freedom songs as they waited for enough bail money to be raised so they could go home.

Parents worried but King promised them that he would look after the children. He told them to be proud of their brave girls and boys who were marching not just for themselves but for all America. The children had filled the jails, and now their story filled the papers and the evening news programs. America and the world looked on in horror.

The pictures from Birmingham explained racism better than any speech could, and people saw it was time for change. Project Confrontation had worked! On May 10,

Birmingham city leaders agreed to free everyone who had been jailed. They also began to desegregate businesses.

President John F. Kennedy also saw that things had to change. On June 11, millions of people turned on their television sets to watch him speak. He said: "One hundred years of delay have passed since President Lincoln freed the slaves, yet their heirs, their grandsons, are not fully free. . . . Now the time has come for this nation to fulfill its promise."

Several days later, the president introduced his plans for what would become the Civil Rights Act of 1964. The act would ban segregation in all public places and make job discrimination based on race illegal. But first it needed enough votes in Congress to become a law.

Civil rights leaders wanted to combine strength in numbers to help build support for the Civil Rights Act. Working together, organizers set their sights on a very important march in the nation's capital: Washington, DC.

Too Scary to Stay

"Things are getting tense in Birmingham," Cousin Charles says. He puts his coffee cup down. "It was bad enough when white people threw food at peaceful protesters and pulled them off their seats at a lunch counter."

Charles's wife, Tish, taps her bright-red fingernails on the table. "It's not just tense. Some of it is dangerous. The police turned dogs and fire hoses on children. *Children!*"

I know what Tish is talking about. Everyone does. It happened last week, and the news of it is still on the TV every night—images of black schoolkids in Birmingham, singing and carrying signs, and then policemen turning giant hoses on them. The blasts of water were so strong that they knocked the children to the ground.

I glance at Val. She's eleven and my favorite cousin. When I got her letter telling me that she and her parents were moving to Detroit, I was so excited. That was before I knew they were moving because things are so dangerous in Birmingham.

Val is staring at her dish of ice cream. "There's always police in the streets and people getting arrested in Birmingham. I knew one of those kids who got knocked down by a water hose. She said it was really scary."

"Wow," I say. "Those kids stood up for themselves. That was really brave."

"I know," Val says. "But we're just kids."

"But we still count," I say. "It's our world, too."

Chapter 7

Planning the March

On July 2, 1963, civil rights activists gathered in New York City. There were members from several important civil rights organizations at the meeting, including Martin Luther King Jr., A. Philip Randolph, and a man named Bayard Rustin. The diverse group worked together to create a list of ten demands for their march, calling it the March on Washington for Jobs and Freedom. They called for equal rights in employment, education, housing, and voting.

Rustin and a group of about two hundred volunteers had only two months to prepare, and there was a lot of work to do! One of the first goals was to raise money—about $100,000. Rustin's volunteers **solicited** church groups and labor unions. They asked celebrities to hold fund-raisers. They sold buttons with an image of a white and a black hand

A woman holds up buttons for the March on Washington

clasped together. People bought the buttons—forty-two thousand in just one month—and the group made nearly $15,000.

With some of the money collected, the volunteers created and mailed thousands of manuals to civil rights organizations and churches. The manuals explained how to prepare for the march and what to do on the day of the march—including where to stay, what to wear, and what to pack in their box lunches. The workers also wrote and distributed pamphlets with information about the march. In one month, they passed out almost four hundred thousand flyers!

Rustin's goal was to get at least one hundred thousand people to come to the march. So, he talked about it as much as he could. He gave speeches and held press conferences. He spoke on the radio and on TV. He gave interviews to newspaper and magazine journalists. Through his hard work, Rustin made sure that almost everyone in America knew about the march. Now, he hoped that lots of them would attend.

Organizers didn't encourage only black people to attend. "The march must be integrated," Randolph said. "The idea of Negroes and whites locked in mortal warfare—that's just not true." Soon people of other races joined in to organize the march.

Some of the money raised was spent on transportation. Over two thousand chartered buses and forty trains were reserved for the event. Shuttle buses were set up to transport people from the Washington, DC, train station to the march site. Money was also needed to set up first aid stations and bathrooms along the march route. Some of the bathrooms were giant trucks with facilities for thirty or forty people.

Security was especially important. The event would be staffed by more than four thousand police officers and members of the National Guard. An additional four thousand army and marine troops would be on call in case additional help was necessary. There were also two thousand marshals, who were trained to control a crowd without force.

Organizers plan the route for the March on Washington

While all of this planning was happening, civil rights leaders were discussing the march with President Kennedy. He did not support the event because he thought the timing was wrong. In response, Martin Luther King Jr. said, "Frankly, I have never engaged in any direct-action movement which did *not* seem ill-timed." When the President realized that the march would go on whether he liked it or not, he publicly announced his support.

Although many women were involved in the civil rights movement, none of them were invited to speak at the event. Only men were included in the program. Wives of the march's leaders were not even allowed to walk alongside their husbands. Female civil rights activists, including Rosa Parks, were asked to walk behind the men. Many women thought this was unfair. They had been fighting for civil rights just as long and as hard as men had.

Anna Arnold Hedgeman, a black woman and the only woman on the march's organizing committee, spoke up. Organizers agreed to add a tribute to the women who had fought for freedom, but they asked a man to deliver the remarks. Hedgeman was outraged. She eventually convinced Randolph that a woman should be the one to speak.

To make sure all the speakers could be heard, Rustin had the best sound system installed. But on August 27, the night before the march, the sound system was **sabotaged**. It was fixed in time, but the act of sabotage rattled the organizers. Would there be more trouble the day of the march? Most importantly, could they keep everyone safe?

Important Work

When I walk into the kitchen, my big sister, Yvonne, is making sandwiches—lots of them. Everything is spread across the kitchen table. "Who are all these sandwiches for?" I ask.

"They're for the group taking the bus trip down to DC," Yvonne says. "We're leaving tonight, and everybody's bringing food to share. Want to help wrap the sandwiches in wax paper?"

I nod. "Are you excited about the march?"

"Yes, I am!" Yvonne's earrings dangle as she nods. "Remember how our cousins were told they couldn't buy the house they wanted because they're black? Nobody has the right to tell you where you can and can't live! If we had open housing laws everywhere, that real estate guy couldn't have done what he did."

I sort of understand. "But how is marching in Washington going to help them get a house in Detroit?"

"Hopefully, there will be thousands of people at the march," Yvonne explains. "A crowd that big will force government officials to listen to black people and change the laws all over the country."

"Will it be as big as the Walk to Freedom? Will Dr. King be there?" I marched with my parents in the Walk to Freedom in Detroit two months ago.

Dr. King gave a speech there that made me feel inspired.

Yvonne smiles. "It might be even bigger! I bet all the TV news programs will cover it. Especially when Dr. King speaks."

I stack a wax-paper-wrapped sandwich on top of four others. "And then you're going back to school." I sigh. "I can't believe the summer's almost over."

"Time goes fast when you're doing important work," Yvonne says, putting her arm around me and giving me a squeeze.

Chapter 8

The People Come and Come and Come

As the sun rose on the morning of August 28, organizers felt excited and nervous. Would people show up? How many?

Nearly two weeks before the march, a group of thirteen teenagers from Brooklyn, New York, started their journey to Washington on foot. They walked more than 230 miles, carrying signs that read, "We March from New York City for Freedom."

The group left from Brooklyn at 5:30 a.m. on August 15. They camped out wherever they could find a spot. One dark night, they tried pitching their tents, but their stakes wouldn't go into the ground. They slept in just their sleeping bags. In the morning, they discovered they had camped out in a supermarket parking lot! "We basically lived off of packaged cookies," sixteen-year-old Lawrence Cumberbatch said. After twelve days, the group arrived in Washington, DC, ready to march.

Teenagers begin their walk from Brooklyn, New York, to Washington, DC

Twenty-seven-year-old Ledger Smith roller-skated seven hundred miles from Chicago to the march. He wore a bright-red sash with the word *Freedom* on it. The trip took ten days. And then there was eighty-two-year-old Jay Hardo, who rode all the way from Dayton, Ohio, on his bicycle with an image of an American eagle on its handlebars!

But at 8:00 a.m. on August 28, Bayard Rustin was worried. Only about fifty marchers had gathered at the starting point, the Washington Monument. Where was everyone?

Many of them were at Union Station. Around 7:30, when the first trains pulled in, people poured out. They came from Chicago, Detroit, Tallahassee, and other cities around the country. Trains arrived every five to ten minutes, and soon the station was crowded with marchers, black and white, carrying their lunches and holding protest signs.

Some marchers took shuttle buses from the train station to the National Mall, a large grass field where the Washington Monument and the Lincoln Memorial are located. Some walked. Strangers became friends as they shared their stories and their reasons for attending the march. Many sang freedom songs and gospel tunes. These songs were something people had in common, and singing together made them feel united.

John Hochheimer was thirteen years old when he boarded a bus in Virginia alone. He listened to others on the bus talk about the violence and segregation they had experienced all over the South. John, the son of Holocaust survivors, said the experience showed him that there was no difference between the evils his Jewish family experienced during the Holocaust and the injustices black people were going through.

The number of marchers gathered around the Washington Monument grew. Well-known singers Bob Dylan, Joan Baez, Mahalia Jackson, and the group Peter, Paul and Mary entertained the crowd. Bystanders joined in with the songs. Ordinary people sang along with famous athletes, musicians, and actors. Baseball player Jackie Robinson; singer Marian Anderson; and actors Sammy Davis Jr., Charlton Heston, Diahann Carroll, and Marlon Brando were there. By 11:00 a.m., nearly one hundred thousand people had gathered. The sun continued to rise higher and higher in the sky. People wearing their Sunday best—men in suits, women in dresses and hats—sweltered in the heat as they waited to march. They were hopeful and excited.

The march's organizers, who were scheduled to lead the crowd to the Lincoln Memorial at 11:30 a.m., were in a meeting in the Capitol. At around 11:20 a.m., some marchers decided to begin walking. As the leaders saw the group start to move, Rustin said, "My God, they're *going!*" The march was starting without them!

Getting to Washington, DC

"Mommy, how long does it take to get to Washington, DC?" My mom and I are up very early. Neither of us got much sleep, wondering if Yvonne and the others made it to the capital.

Mommy looks at me over her coffee cup. "They should be there by now."

As I pour milk into my cereal, I wonder how Vonnie is feeling right now. Just then, the phone rings.

I jump up to answer it before mommy can, sending my spoon clattering to the floor.

"Vonnie!" I shout. I hear a funny noise as Yvonne drops more coins into the pay phone she's using.

"Dee Dee?" Her voice sounds muffled.

"Vonnie, are you in DC yet? What's happening?"

"Yes, we're here. It's wild! There are so many buses that we had to park in this long line and walk to where the march is starting. There must be thousands of folks here already. And they're from everywhere!"

"What do you mean, everywhere?"

"Well, so far I've seen buses from California and Louisiana, and I just heard someone speaking with a British accent," Yvonne explains. "Seems like our calls for equal rights in America have been heard across the world."

Chapter 9

The March on Washington for Jobs and Freedom

Rustin hurried to his spot along with the other march leaders and joined the crowd. The marchers took two routes leading to the Lincoln Memorial. By noon, the National Mall was a sea of people.

Eleven-year-old Odehyah Gough-Israel remembered walking down the Mall with her thirteen-year-old sister. "I think what impressed me the most were the freedom songs," she said. "We take it for granted now, but when we sang, 'We Shall Overcome,' it was with such fervor, such great emotion . . .

It was a day of pride, even at my age; it was a day that we really felt empowered."

As the crowd moved, TV cameras followed. In 1963, it was rare for TV stations to broadcast live for many hours in a row, but on this day, one network canceled all of its other programs so that it could broadcast the entire march. Millions of people around the world were about to watch the historic event live in their homes.

People filled every inch of the Mall between the Washington Monument and the Lincoln Memorial. The sun reflected off the pool. It was now after 2:00 p.m., and it was time for the scheduled program to begin.

After the National Anthem was sung, A. Philip Randolph gave the opening remarks. As he gazed at the crowd he said, "We here, today, are only the first wave. When we leave, it will be to carry the civil rights revolution home with us into every nook and cranny of the land."

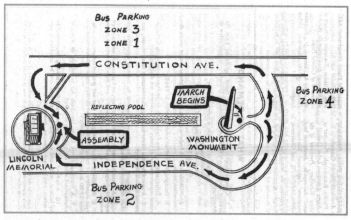

A map from a program handed out at the march

Daisy Gatson Bates, a civil rights activist, presented the "Tribute to Negro Women Fighters for Freedom" that Anna Arnold Hedgeman had fought so hard to include. Then Randolph slowly called out the names of the five women honored, including Rosa Parks. Bates finished the tribute by saying, "We will kneel-in, we will sit-in, until we can eat in any counter in the United States. We will walk until we are free, until we can walk to any school and take our children to any school in the United States." Although Bates didn't have much time to speak, she used the moment to spread a powerful message: Women were an important part of the civil rights movement and could not be overlooked.

When twenty-three-year-old John Lewis, the youngest speaker of the day, came to the podium, he was nervous. He was afraid that he wouldn't be able to speak in front of such a large crowd. But he did, and his words were fiery. "To those who have said, 'Be patient and wait,' we must say that we cannot be patient. We do not want our freedom gradually, but we want to be free now. We are tired. . . . How long can we be patient? We want our freedom and we want it now." Several times, his speech was interrupted by applause.

As the day wore on, many people became hot, tired, and restless. Some tried to seek shelter under the shade of the trees that bordered the Mall. Others cooled off in the reflecting pool. Still others packed up and went home, unable to stand in the heat any

Leaders of the march with protest signs

longer. Then gospel singer Mahalia Jackson took the stage and performed two songs. As her voice boomed, people in the crowd swayed, clapped, and sang along. Jackson's songs revitalized the crowd as they stood together, as one.

At last, the speaker whom most people were anticipating was called to the podium: Dr. Martin Luther King Jr. The crowd greeted him with wild applause and cheers. For a full minute, he gazed out upon the people who had come to hear him speak.

Dr. King's strong, deep voice boomed across the Mall. His words touched everyone's hearts. He reminded the crowd that the Emancipation Proclamation promised freedom for all African Americans. Yet, one hundred years later, this promise had not been fulfilled. Still, he told the people not to be bitter, not to hate. He called out for justice. He called out for equality. He called out for civil rights.

At one point during the speech, Mahalia Jackson called to Martin Luther King, "Tell them about the dream, Martin!" So Martin Luther King strayed from his script—and what he said next would become some of the most memorable lines ever spoken: "I have a dream. . . . I have a dream that my four little children will one day live in a nation where they will not be judged by the color of their skin but by the content of their character." His dream was that one day people of every race and religion would be able to get along and work and live together.

As people listened to Dr. King's powerful words, some sobbed. Others nodded their heads and shouted in agreement. Rosetta Canada-Hargrove, who was twenty years old when she attended the march, remembered that when Dr. King started talking, everyone was silent. She said, "You didn't hear babies crying or anything. It was just still. And the momentum that started to build up, you saw people crying. I was crying. And you saw people, strangers, black and white, hugging each other."

Another face in the crowd was Edith Lee-Payne from Detroit, Michigan. She celebrated her twelfth birthday by going to the march with her mother. "It was important for my mother to be there," Edith later said. "And being her one and only child, it was important for me to be there with her." Edith's mother had been in show business. Edith listened as her mother discussed things that Edith had never heard her speak about before, such as having to enter hotels through the back door, while the white performers entered through the front. As Edith listened to Dr. King's speech, she felt "glad to be standing with people that wanted to make things right."

Edith Lee-Payne at the march

Photographer Rowland Scherman was taking pictures that day. He saw people laughing. He saw people crying. And then he saw Edith in the front row, watching King's speech. She looked so *involved*. He snapped her photo. The picture of this young girl became famous, appearing in documentaries, textbooks, and museum exhibits.

At 4:30 p.m., the march was over. People got back into their cars, boarded buses and trains, hopped on their bicycles and motor-cycles, and headed back home. As A. Philip Randolph watched everyone leave, tears filled his eyes. He later told his friends this had been "the most beautiful and glorious day" of his life.

Melody

A Day to Remember

Yvonne goes right back to college after the march, but a few days later I get a big envelope in the mail. I'm excited as I rip it open. Out falls a postcard and a letter. I unfold the letter, which is scrawled on lined notebook paper. Yvonne's handwriting is usually very neat, but this is messy, like she was writing fast. Then I realize that Vonnie has sent me a diary of her day. I start to read out loud.

"10 a.m. We were starving, because we ate all of our sandwiches on the bus. But we met some other students from Howard University here in Washington. They showed us where to eat cheap!

So many college students here, ready for change!

"It's so hot already that my blouse is sticking to my back.

"11 a.m. Somebody said there are movie stars and famous people here. I've only seen lots of newspaper and TV reporters. I think this march is going to be famous!

"12 Noon. Everyone's starting to march toward the National Mall! We're shoulder to shoulder, but even strangers are polite and friendly. I can see the Lincoln Memorial where the speakers are—but it looks really far away . . ."

I stop reading and stare at the postcard. There's a big white building with lots of steps and tall columns. Between the columns I can see a giant statue of President Abraham Lincoln. It's the Lincoln Memorial. I look back at Vonnie's letter. The rest of it is scribbled and even harder to read, as if she's trying to hurry and tell me everything without missing anything that was going on.

"Miss Mahalia Jackson's gospel singing makes me feel tingly all over. We clapped so much that she sang two songs instead of one.

"Oh, Reverend King just finished! At first it sounded like the speech he gave at the Walk to Freedom in Detroit. But it wasn't. We all chanted with him: 'Free at last! Free at last!'"

I imagine thousands of people coming together to march for equality and justice. I imagine Dr. King at the top of the steps of the Lincoln Memorial, and I imagine Yvonne raising her sign and cheering the speakers, and chanting with Dr. King.

I know from reading her letter that Yvonne will never forget that day. I wasn't there with her, but I feel like I was. I won't ever forget that day, either.

Chapter 10

Success and Sorrow

The March on Washington for Jobs and Freedom became one of the most famous moments in history. It broke the record for the largest civil rights demonstration, with more than two hundred and fifty thousand people. About 70 percent were black, and about 30 percent were white or other races. They were all there with a shared goal: equality for everyone. Remarkably, there was no violence. It was peaceful. Those who walked, stood, and sang together in the nation's capital felt a deep sense of unity.

Around the world, thousands of people watched live coverage of the march on TV. For many people, it was the first time they had ever seen Martin Luther King Jr. speak. Like those at the march, people at home were also moved by what they saw. One white woman from Atlanta, Georgia, said, "I haven't been for this civil rights stuff and I've never liked King. But I watched him on TV, and after it was over I was proud of the Negro and proud of America. . . . He made my country seem so beautiful I felt like I wanted to shake his hand."

Carrying out an organized, peaceful protest was one goal of the march. Another was to press Congress to pass the civil rights bill. But in some parts of the country, people were not in favor of this legislation. The governors of Alabama and Mississippi called it the "civil wrongs" bill. They and other southern lawmakers debated and delayed the bill for months, keeping it from going to a vote.

Supporters of the bill waited with a sense of hope. The march had brought together people of many races, genders, and backgrounds, and many believed that harmony would win over hatred. But less than three weeks after the march, an act of racial violence shocked the world. **White supremacists** bombed the Sixteenth Street Baptist Church in Birmingham. Four young black girls were killed. Two months later, in November 1963, President John F. Kennedy was assassinated. Both horrific events shook the country's feelings of hope and unity.

Vice President Lyndon B. Johnson, who became president after Kennedy's death, worked hard to pass the civil rights bill. On July 2, 1964, the Civil Rights Act became a law. It outlawed discrimination in all public places such as hotels, restaurants, gas stations, and theaters, required that public schools no longer be segregated, and made it illegal for employers to discriminate based on race, religion, gender, sexual orientation, or national origin.

The front page of a newspaper after President Kennedy was shot

Although discrimination was now illegal, things did not change overnight. Civil rights activists continued their work of civil disobedience, economic protests, and legal battles. In 1965, the Voting Rights Act was passed, preventing states from making people pass literacy tests before they could vote. It took until April 11, 1968, to pass the Fair Housing

President Lyndon B. Johnson shakes Dr. Martin Luther King Jr.'s hand at the signing of the Civil Rights Act

Act, making it illegal to discriminate when renting or selling property.

Dr. Martin Luther King Jr. never saw the Fair Housing Act enacted, as he was tragically assassinated in Memphis, Tennessee, on April 4, 1968. The civil rights movement lost one of its strongest voices, yet other activists knew they had to continue. The progress that had been made through courageous acts of civil disobedience would lead the way for new generations to continue fighting inequality. And the historic March on Washington for Jobs and Freedom, with its powerful messages of hope and unity, would never be forgotten.

"I can't believe it," my cousin Val suddenly says, as we walk along a street in Birmingham, Alabama, with my older sister Yvonne.

"What is it?" I ask. All I see are a bunch of stores.

"The sign is gone!" Val says, stopping in the middle of the sidewalk. She points to the ice-cream parlor at the end of the block. "Before we moved to Detroit, there was a sign in this window that read 'Whites Only.' Like a lot of businesses around here, they refused to serve black customers."

I turn to Yvonne. "But that's against the law now, isn't it?"

She nods. "The president signed the Civil Rights Act. Now everyone, no matter what color, has an equal right to stores and restaurants and movie theaters and schools and buses and jobs."

"So that means we can shop anywhere now?" Val asks.

"Yes. That's the new law," Yvonne answers.

"Let's go get some ice cream," I say. Yvonne and I start walking, but Val hangs back.

"What if they still won't serve us?" Val asks, frowning.

"They have to, Val," Yvonne says. "And I believe they will."

"Me, too," I say, linking my arm in Val's.

"I think no sign *is* a sign. Things are changing."

Yvonne smiles. "That's right, Dee Dee!"

"Let's go in!" I say.

As we enter the shop, I feel like this moment is about more than ice cream. It's about justice and fairness and more changes that will keep making things better.

Epilogue

Although many laws have been passed that make it illegal to discriminate based on race, discrimination and racism still exist in the United States.

As an adult, Edith Lee-Payne, the little girl who became the face of the March on Washington, said that her dream of equal rights began to fade. "I was denied employment at least fifty times, only—*only*—because I was black. As soon as I'd walk through the door, and the employer would see me, I would be told that the job had already been filled, or

I probably wouldn't like the job anyway, or they need to reschedule something. . . . Instead of seeing the equality and the justice and the freedom and jobs that we should really have fifty years later, it's not there in a lot of places."

On August 28, 2013—the fiftieth anniversary of the march—Edith once again spent her birthday in Washington at the Lincoln Memorial. "There's no place that I could be, other than there," she said. "It's too personal for me."

Today, people continue to fight for civil rights. Black, white, Latinx, Native American. People from different religions. Men and women. Gay people and straight people. Young and old. Leaders and everyday citizens. Americans have not stopped demonstrating, protesting, boycotting, sitting in, and standing up for equality.

Glossary

Boycott – to join others in refusing to support a person, organization, or business as a way of protesting

Civil disobedience – the refusal to follow laws or demands as a nonviolent form of protest

Civil rights – the rights every person should have, no matter his or her race, gender, ethnicity, religion, or sexual orientation

Discrimination – when a person or a group is treated unfairly, often because of race, gender, ethnicity, religion, or sexual orientation

Economic protest – withholding money from an organization or business to force a change

Emancipation Proclamation – President Lincoln's 1863 declaration that all enslaved people in the Confederate states were free

Jim Crow laws – laws in the South from the 1870s to the 1950s that discriminated against black people

Literacy – the ability to read and write

Prejudice – an opinion or judgment formed about a specific group without knowledge or reason

Racism – when someone is treated badly just because of their race

Sabotaged – damaged or interfered with

Segregated – separated

Solicit – to ask or plea

Union – an organization of workers formed to improve conditions for all workers

White supremacist – a person who believes that white people are better than all other races

Source Notes

Anderson, Jessica Cumberbatch. "March on Washington 1963: Eyewitnesses to History Look Back." *Huffington Post*, August 27, 2013; updated December 6, 2017, https://www.huffingtonpost.com/2013/08/27/march-on-washington-eyewitnesses-to-history-photos_n_3792414.html.

Aretha, David. *Martin Luther King Jr. and the 1963 March on Washington*. Greensboro, North Carolina: Morgan Reynolds Publishing, 2013.

"At 1963 March, A Face in the Crowd Became a Poster Child." Michele Norris, correspondent. National Public Radio, *Morning Edition*, August 21, 2013, https://www.npr.org/2013/08/21/213804335/at-1963-march-a-face-in-the-crowd-became-a-poster-child.

"Birmingham and the Children's March." Kim Lawton, correspondent. *Religion & Ethics Newsweekly*, PBS, April 26, 2013, http://www.pbs.org/wnet/religionandethics/2013/04/26/april-26-2013-birmingham-and-the-childrens-march/16051/.

Branch, Taylor. *Parting the Waters: America in the King Years 1954–63*. New York: Simon & Schuster, 1988.

Burrow, Rufus. *A Child Shall Lead Them: Martin Luther King Jr., Young People and the Movement*. Minneapolis: Fortress Press, 2014.

Carson, Clayborne, David J. Garrow, Gerald Gill, Vincent Harding, and Darlene Clark Hine, eds. *The Eyes on the Prize Civil Rights Reader: Documents, Speeches, and Firsthand Accounts from the Black Freedom Struggle, 1954–1990*. New York: Penguin Books, 1991.

Chafe, William H. *Civilities and Civil Rights: Greensboro, North Carolina, and the Black Struggle for Freedom*. Oxford: Oxford University Press, 1980.

DeVinney, James, A., Julian Bond, and Henry Hampton, *Eyes on the Prize: America's Civil Rights Years, 1954–1965*. Alexandria, VA: PBS Home Video, 2010.

Doak, Robin S. *The March on Washington: Uniting against Racism*. Minneapolis: Compass Point Books, 2008.

Dudziak, Mary L. *Cold War Civil Rights: Race and the Image of American Democracy*. Princeton: Princeton University Press, 2000.

Euchner, Charles. *Nobody Turn Me Around: A People's History of the 1963 March on Washington*. Boston: Beacon Press, 2010.

Gray, Eliza. "Before Rosa Parks, There Was Claudette Colvin." *Newsweek*, March 1, 2009, https://www.newsweek.com/rosa-parks -there-was-claudette-colvin-76163.

Halberstam, David. *The Children*. New York: Fawcett Books, 1998.

Joiner, Lottie L. "How the Children of Birmingham Changed the Civil-Rights Movement." *Daily Beast*, May 2, 2013, https://www .thedailybeast.com/how-the-children-of-birmingham-changed -the-civil-rights-movement.

Jones, Clarence B. and Stuart Connelly, *Behind the Dream: The Making of the Speech that Transformed a Nation*. New York: Palgrave Macmillan, 2013.

Jones, William P. *The March on Washington: Jobs, Freedom, and the Forgotten History of Civil Rights*. New York: W. W. Norton & Company, 2013.

Kasher, Steven. *The Civil Rights Movement: A Photographic History, 1954–68*. New York: Abbeville Press, 1996.

Levingston, Steven. *Kennedy and King: The President, the Pastor, and the Battle over Civil Rights*. New York: Hachette Books, 2017.

Mai, Lina. "'I Had a Right to Be at Central': Remembering Little Rock's Integration Battle." *Time*, September 22, 2017, http://time .com/4948704/little-rock-nine-anniversary/.

"Planning the March on Washington." *Newsweek*, January 19, 2015, https://www.newsweek.com/planning-march-washington-300305.

"Remembering Jim Crow: Children of Jim Crow." By Stephen Smith, Katie Ellis, and Sasha Aslanian, *American Radio Works*, November 2001, http://americanradioworks.publicradio.org /features/remembering/children.html.

Schwartz, Heather E. *The March on Washington: A Primary Source Exploration of the Pivotal Protest.* North Mankato, Minnesota: Capstone Press: 2015.

Watson, Stephanie. *Martin Luther King Jr. and the March on Washington.* Minneapolis: Abdo Publishing, 2016.

Williams, Juan. *Eyes on the Prize: America's Civil Rights Years, 1954–1965.* 1987. Reprint, New York: Penguin, 2013.

"Witnesses to History, 50 Years Later." *New York Times*, August 23, 2013, http://www.nytimes.com/interactive/2013/08/23/us/march -on-washington-anniversary-memories.html.

Timeline

1619 – The first enslaved people are brought to America from Africa

1776 – The United States becomes an official country with the signing of the Declaration of Independence

1861 – The Civil War begins between the Union army (Northern "free states") and Confederate army (Southern "slave states")

1863 – President Lincoln issues the Emancipation Proclamation, declaring all enslaved people in Southern states free

1865 – The Civil War ends and slavery is legally outlawed in Southern states

1909 – The National Association for the Advancement of Colored People (NAACP) is formed

1925 – A. Philip Randolph founds the Brotherhood of Sleeping Car Porters

1954 – The *Brown v. Board of Education* case determines that school segregation is illegal

August 28, 1955 – Emmett Till is kidnapped, beaten, shot, and thrown in a river in Mississippi

December 1, 1955 – Rosa Parks refuses to give up her seat for a white man on a public bus, inspiring a boycott of Montgomery city buses

1957 – The Little Rock Nine are the first black students to attend Central High School in Little Rock, Arkansas

1960 – Four college students sit at the whites-only Woolworth's lunch counter in Greensboro, North Carolina, to protest segregation

May 1963 – Martin Luther King Jr. and the Southern Christian Leadership Conference (SCLC) lead the Children's Crusade march in Birmingham, Alabama

June 23, 1963 – Martin Luther King Jr. leads the Walk to Freedom in Detroit, Michigan

August 28, 1963 – The March on Washington for Jobs and Freedom is held in the nation's capital

September 15, 1963 – The Sixteenth Street Baptist Church is bombed in Birmingham, Alabama

November 22, 1963 – President Kennedy is assassinated in Dallas, Texas

1964 – The Civil Rights Act outlaws discrimination in public places and makes it illegal for employers to discriminate based on race, religion, gender, sexual orientation, or national origin

1965 – The Voting Rights Act prevents states from making people pass literacy tests before they can vote

April 4, 1968 – Martin Luther King Jr. is assassinated in Memphis, Tennessee

1968 – The Fair Housing Act makes it illegal to discriminate when renting or selling property